AMERICAN EXPERIENCE

HOW TO USE YOUR SD-X READER WITH THIS BOOK

This highly interactive book lets you explore the milestones, movements, and people that shaped American history in an interactive format. You can read the book and study the photographs, maps, and illustrations, but a touch of the SD-X Reader adds in-depth audio information and learning games to the page.

1. Press the Power button to turn the SD-X Reader on or off. The LED will light up when the SD-X Reader is on.

2. Touch the volume buttons found on this page or on the Contents page to adjust the volume.

3. Touch photographs and illustrations to hear additional information. Page headers and words or phrases that are in a different size or color than the surrounding text often provide a definition or more information.

4. As you explore the page, you'll encounter games and quizzes. Touch the text or image that started the game to stop playing.

5. After two minutes of inactivity, the Reader will beep and go to sleep.

6. If the batteries are low, the Reader will beep twice and the LED will start blinking. Replace the batteries by following the instructions on the next page. The SD-X Reader uses two AAA batteries.

7. To use headphones or earbuds, plug them into the headphone jack on the bottom of the SD-X Reader.

CHANGE THE VOLUME WITH THESE BUTTONS

UP   DOWN

Battery Information
Interactive Pen includes 2 replaceable AAA batteries (UM-4 or LR03).

Battery Installation
1. Open battery door with small flat-head or Phillips screwdriver.
2. Install new batteries according to +/- polarity. If batteries are not installed properly, the device will not function.
3. Replace battery door; secure with small screw.

Battery Safety
Batteries must be replaced by adults only. Properly dispose of used batteries. Do not dispose of batteries in fire; batteries may explode or leak. See battery manufacturer for disposal recommendations. Do not mix alkaline, standard (carbon-zinc), or rechargeable (nickel-cadmium) batteries. Do not mix old and new batteries. Only recommended batteries of the same or equivalent type should be used. Remove weakened or dead batteries. Never short-circuit the supply terminals. Non-rechargeable batteries are not to be recharged. Do not use rechargeable batteries. If batteries are swallowed, in the USA, promptly see a doctor and have the doctor phone 1-202-625-3333 collect. In other countries, have the doctor call your local poison control center. Batteries should be changed when sounds mix, distort, or become otherwise unintelligible as batteries weaken. The electrostatic discharge may interfere with the sound module. If this occurs, please simply restart the product.

In Europe, the dustbin symbol indicates that batteries, rechargeable batteries, button cells, battery packs, and similar materials must not be discarded in household waste. Batteries containing hazardous substances are harmful to the environment and to health. Please help to protect the environment from health risks by telling your children to dispose of batteries properly and by taking batteries to local collection points. Batteries handled in this manner are safely recycled.

Warning: Changes or modifications to this unit not expressly approved by the party responsible for compliance could void the user's authority to operate the equipment.

NOTE: This equipment has been tested and found to comply with the limits for a Class B digital device, pursuant to Part 15 of the FCC Rules. These limits are designed to provide reasonable protection against harmful interference in a residential installation. This equipment generates, uses, and can radiate radio frequency energy and, if not installed and used in accordance with the instructions, may cause harmful interference to radio communications. However, there is no guarantee that interference will not occur in a particular installation. If this equipment does cause harmful interference to radio or television reception, which can be determined by turning the equipment off and on, the user is encouraged to try to correct the interference by one or more of the following measures: Reorient or relocate the receiving antenna. Increase the separation between the equipment and receiver. Connect the equipment into an outlet on a circuit different from that to which the receiver is connected. Consult the dealer or an experienced radio TV technician for help.

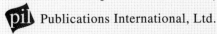 Publications International, Ltd.

Customer service: customer_service@pubint.com

ISBN: 978-1-68022-386-6

Manufactured in China.

8 7 6 5 4 3 2 1

CONTENTS

CHANGE THE VOLUME
WITH THESE BUTTONS

UP

DOWN

AMERICAN ORIGINS

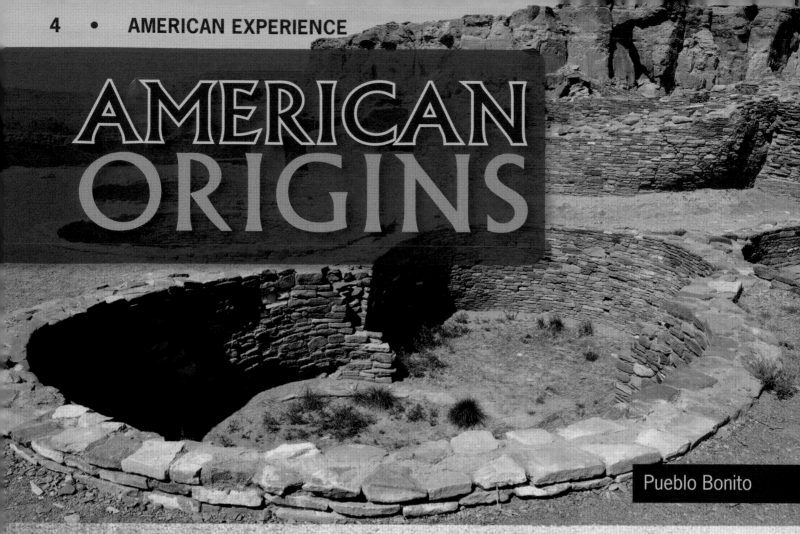

Pueblo Bonito

When the United States became an independent nation in 1776, different peoples had lived on its lands for centuries. Christopher Columbus's arrival in the Americas in 1492 began a new era of exploration, settlement, and exchange in what Europeans saw as a new world.

NATIVE SOCIETIES
Societies of indigenous peoples had lived in North America for thousands of years before the arrival of Europeans. French colonists used the phrase "infinity of nations" in the early 1600s. They recognized that the Americas were populated by many distinct cultures— each with its own language, history, laws, and territory—that were in fact nations.

SOUTHWEST
The Ancestral Puebloans lived in the Four Corners region of the Southwest in what are now Colorado, New Mexico, Arizona, and Utah. Pueblo Bonito was an ancient settlement and was a major center for Ancestral Puebloan culture and trade.

GREAT LAKES
The Great Lakes region was home to many diverse Native peoples, including the Anishinaabe. In the 1790s, the Anishinaabe traded goods with the British and other Native peoples who lived or hunted in the region, including the Dakota to the west, Cree to the north, Huron to the east, and Potawatomi to the south.

WHAT YEAR?

PLAINS

The Indian nations of the Plains were located in a vast, flat region covered with prairies and low, rolling hills known as the Great Plains. In the 1800s, one of these nations, the Apsáalooke, lived in prime buffalo-hunting territory in present-day Montana.

EARLY SETTLEMENTS

Three settlements, established by England, France, and Spain in the early 1600s, created a new world for both the settlers and the original inhabitants in the territory being colonized.

JAMESTOWN

English adventurers chose the Chesapeake region for the Jamestown settlement partly because it was home of the powerful Powhatan people, from whom they expected to get food and possibly tribute in valuable goods. The English settlers of 1607 were mostly military men, prepared to explore, deal with the Indians, and seek out riches of the area. They were not prepared to grow crops or fish the waterways themselves, so when they found survival difficult, they raided Powhatan villages for corn.

QUÉBEC

For decades, French ships had traveled to the Gulf of St. Lawrence, where they fished the waters and traded for furs with Native people on the riverbanks. In 1608, French settlers established Québec to pursue the lucrative fur trade. They allied with Montagnais, Algonkin, and Huron peoples, who were leading traders from deep in the interior. The alliance brought the French great profits, but also a century of conflict with the powerful Iroquois confederacy south of the Great Lakes.

American Bison

SANTA FE

In 1598, Spanish conquistador Juan de Oñate led an expedition of soldiers and settlers into New Mexico in hopes of finding rich mines and rich lands. Oñate expected the people he called Pueblos—actually independent groups with different languages and societies—to supply the labor for exploiting the resources of the region. Oñate found no silver or gold, but Franciscan missionaries found a reason for maintaining a settlement in the area: converting the Pueblos to Christianity.

What was the Pueblo Revolt of 1680?

Where was the oldest continuing European settlement in the United States?

1492   1565   1607   1620   1680

COLONIAL AMERICA

Over four centuries ago, English adventurers built a fort on the James River near the Chesapeake Bay. In the decades after 1607, shipload after shipload of colonists sought new lives in North America. They began moving inland, settling along the coastal rivers of Virginia and Maryland. These early immigrants left us dramatic evidence of their lives— in the traces of the structures they built, the foods they ate, the objects they used, and in their unmarked graves and skeletons.

Jamestown National Historic Site

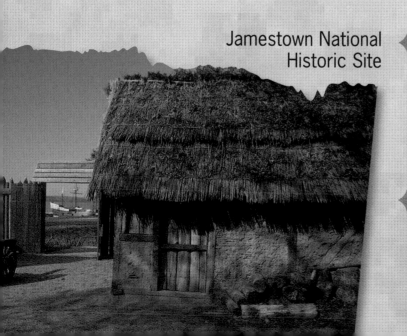

In colonial Virginia and Maryland, much of the economy revolved around tobacco.

THE STARVING TIME

Until recently, little was known about the first inhabitants of Jamestown or their first home, James Fort. Then archaeologists began to find their graves. By studying these skeletons, investigators now grasp more fully what happened to them. Most of the colonists who fought for a foothold in Jamestown died during its first three years.

Colonists wrote about the brutal winter "Starving Time" of 1609–1610, when by one account, only 60 Virginia settlers survived out of 500. In the face of slow death by starvation, a few of the desperate resorted to living off the remains of the dead. These written accounts had never been proven until recently. The bones found in a trash deposit within the James Fort site confirm this grisly period of survival.

Can you name the 13 original colonies that formed the United States?

COLONIAL QUIZ

YES
NO

The first recorded arrival of Africans in English America had occurred by 1619.

REASONS FOR REBELLION

When the French and Indian War ended in 1763, conflict and tension grew between Great Britain and its colonies. Colonists bristled when the British government began enacting taxes and other binding laws, including the Stamp Act, without deference to colonial governments. Colonists issued statements of their rights, appealed to the king and people of Britain, petitioned Parliament, boycotted British goods, and harassed royal officials. The years 1764–1775 saw repeated clashes between Britain and its American colonies. Finally, in 1776, America declared independence from Britain.

What was the Stamp Act?

BOSTON MASSACRE

On March 5, 1770, British soldiers fired into a crowd that had been pelting them with insults and snowballs. Five colonists were killed. Paul Revere's portrayal of the event—with a line of soldiers firing when an officer gave the order—was intentionally inaccurate, designed to arouse public outrage.

REVOLUTIONARY WAR

Americans went to war in 1775 to win their independence from Great Britain. Just weeks after the outbreak of fighting at Lexington and Concord, Congress appointed George Washington general and commander in chief of an army "for the Defense of American Liberty." Outmatched American troops often retreated, but returned to fight again, frustrating British efforts to crush the rebellion. A stunning American victory at Yorktown sapped Britain's will to fight.

CONTINENTAL FORCES

In June 1775, the Continental Congress united the troops of the several colonies into a single Continental army under the command of General George Washington. The men of Washington's army were young and mostly poor farmers, fishermen, and artisans; some were Africans. All were volunteers, although many joined for a cash award.

LEXINGTON AND CONCORD

On April 19, 1775, British troops in Boston marched in darkness toward nearby Concord to seize the local militia's cache of arms and gunpowder. Patriots from Boston alerted the countryside. At dawn, the British confronted a militia unit gathered on the green in Lexington. During the standoff, a shot was fired. In a brief melee, eight colonists were killed and ten were wounded.

From Lexington, British troops marched to Concord, where they destroyed the few supplies the militia had not hidden. After a fierce skirmish with militia, they started back to Boston. Hundreds of militiamen joined the counterattack, forcing the British to make a desperate retreat. Exhausted and panicked, British soldiers lashed out, killing civilians, ransacking and looting houses, and setting fires.

News of the fighting at Lexington and Concord rallied "Friends of American Liberty" in all the colonies. Some colonists recoiled from the notion of taking up arms. Others joined the fight resolved to save themselves and their children from lives of "perpetual slavery" under British rule. The war for independence had begun.

George Washington

VICTORY AT YORKTOWN

In the fall of 1781, Washington's army, with French support, trapped British forces at York-town, Virginia. They bombarded the town relentlessly and, in bold assaults, captured important outlying positions. Fierce British counterattacks proved fruitless. On October 17, the British commander, Lord Charles Cornwallis, surrendered, ending the military phase of the Revolutionary War.

Battle of Lexington   British surrender at Yorktown

FROM REVOLUTION TO CONSTITUTION

CONTINENTAL CONGRESS

The nation's first governing body was the Continental Congress, formed in 1774. The Second Continental Congress included representatives from each state and was designed to be weak. The former colonists were fearful of centralized authority. The Second Continental Congress established the Articles of Confederation that were ratified in 1781.

CONSTITUTIONAL CONVENTION

In 1787, delegates from every state except Rhode Island met at Independence Hall in Philadelphia, Pennsylvania, to rewrite the Articles of Confederation. The delegates debated about how much power to allow the central government, how many representatives in Congress to allow each state, and how these representatives would be elected. In the end, they created a new form of government, with three branches and checks and balances among them.

TIMELINE MATCH

Touch a year on the left. Then touch the matching event on the right.

1774 1781	British surrender at Yorktown
	Declaration of Independence signed
1775 1783	First Continental Congress convenes in Philadelphia
	Treaty of Paris signed
1776 1787	Revolutionary War begins
	Constitutional Convention meets and writes U.S. Constitution

SLAVERY

Slavery in America was big business. On the eve of the Civil War, four million slaves produced cash crops—cotton, tobacco, and rice—that were exported at high prices. In addition to the crops they raised, slaves themselves were commodities to be bought, sold, bred, and borrowed against.

THE MIDDLE PASSAGE

Crossing the Atlantic in the hold of a slave ship was a horrific ordeal. Perhaps one-third of the captives perished on this journey, known as the Middle Passage—the middle leg of a three-part trade in slaves and goods between Europe, Africa, and the Americas.

Sailors packed people together below decks. Standing was impossible, and even rolling over was often difficult. Poor ventilation, dampness, heat, cold, seasickness, rats, poor food, and a lack of sanitation left the conditions squalid, suffocating, and deadly. Outbreaks of disease spread quickly among captives and crew.

RESISTANCE AND REVOLT

Enslaved people on the Middle Passage were not simply passive captives. Some refused to eat and had to be fed against their will. Others threw themselves overboard rather than submit to slavery.

TRUE OR FALSE

T

F

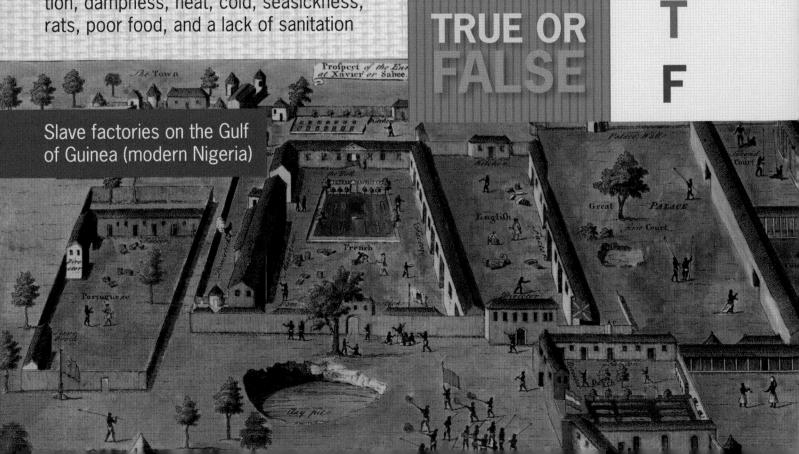

Slave factories on the Gulf of Guinea (modern Nigeria)

THOMAS JEFFERSON AND SLAVERY

Thomas Jefferson drafted the Declaration of Independence and helped create a new nation based on individual freedom and self-government. Jefferson called slavery an "abominable crime," yet he was a lifelong slaveholder. Jefferson and other founders who opposed slavery did not insist on abolishing it. It took 87 more years—and the Civil War, the Emancipation Proclamation, and the Thirteenth Amendment—to end slavery.

How many presidents owned slaves?

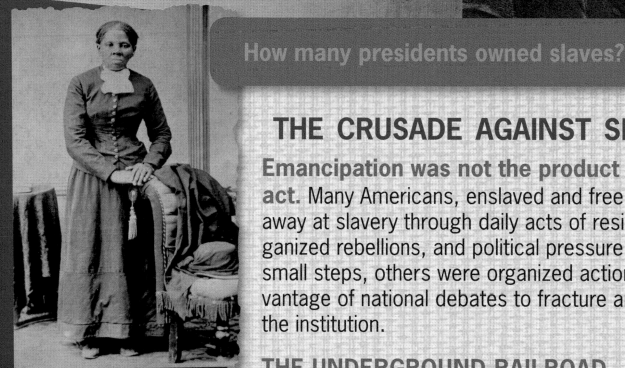

Harriet Tubman

THE CRUSADE AGAINST SLAVERY

Emancipation was not the product of one act. Many Americans, enslaved and free, chipped away at slavery through daily acts of resistance, organized rebellions, and political pressure. Some were small steps, others were organized actions taking advantage of national debates to fracture and destroy the institution.

THE UNDERGROUND RAILROAD

During the 1800s, thousands of enslaved black Southerners ran away from their owners. They followed secret routes known as the Underground Railroad as they traveled north toward free states and Canada or south to Mexico. Slaves who tried to escape risked punishment, being caught and returned to slavery, or even being killed.

SLAVE REBELLIONS

Slave rebellions carried bloody consequences. Rebels were executed. Family, friends, and neighbors might be beaten and killed. Nevertheless, against terrible odds, enslaved people rebelled. Slave uprisings in the South, most notably Nat Turner's rebellion in Virginia in 1831, dramatically underscored the risks slaves would incur themselves to break their chains of bondage.

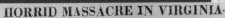

HORRID MASSACRE IN VIRGINIA

Nat Turner's Rebellion

LEWIS AND

In 1803, President Thomas Jefferson commissioned the Corps of Discovery expedition under the leadership of Meriwether Lewis and William Clark to explore the Missouri River and routes to the Pacific Ocean. Their mission was to travel from the mouth of the Missouri River, near St. Louis, to the Pacific Ocean, and back again. For 28 months they explored the American Northwest, mapping rivers, collecting plants and animals new to science, holding councils with Native Americans, and keeping detailed journals.

JEFFERSON'S INSTRUCTIONS

The main objective of the expedition, as stated by Thomas Jefferson in his official instructions, was to find "the most direct and practicable water communication across this continent, for the purposes of commerce." But along the way they were also to learn of the "language, traditions, monuments" of the Indian tribes; to study the "animals of the country generally" and "mineral productions of every kind"; and to determine longitude and latitude by making "celestial observations."

Meriwether Lewis

BY THE NUMBERS

11

820,000

15

1

28

8,000

NEW KNOWLEDGE

While the expedition failed to find an easy water route across the country, the Corps of Discovery returned with a great deal of knowledge about the new United States territory west of the Mississippi—the people, the land, the rivers, the mountains, the plants, and the animals. The maps developed during and after the expedition included a greatly expanded view of the Rocky Mountains and a more accurate positioning of some of the western rivers.

CLARK

How much did the Louisiana Purchase cost?

William Clark

MAPPING A NEW TERRITORY

At the time of the expedition, the United States of America had just acquired from France the vast area of the North American interior known as the Louisiana Territory. The new territory from the Louisiana Purchase included much of what are now the states of Montana, Wyoming, North Dakota, South Dakota, Colorado, Nebraska, Kansas, Minnesota, Iowa, Missouri, New Mexico, Texas, Oklahoma, Arkansas, and Louisiana. The Corps of Discovery expedition made important contributions to the mapping of the North American continent.

Lewis and Clark with Sacagawea, her husband, Toussaint Charbonneau, and their baby, Jean-Baptiste

INTO INDIAN COUNTRY

The Louisiana Purchase nearly doubled the territorial size of the United States. Occupying that vast area were numerous Indian tribes. During their journey, Lewis and Clark made contact with various Indian tribes, many of which provided crucial help to the expedition, including the Mandans, Hidatsa, Shoshone, and Nez Percé Indians.

Lewis and Clark discovered that the Rocky Mountains were much more extensive and rough than expected.

WAR OF 1812

America went to war against Great Britain to assert its rights as an independent, sovereign nation, and to attempt the conquest of Canada. The United States achieved few of its goals and the war ended in a stalemate.

REASONS FOR WAR

The United States had many reasons for going to war in 1812:

- Britain's interference with international trade and impressment of American seamen
- Americans' desire to expand settlement into Indian, British, and Spanish territories
- Aspirations to conquer Canada and end British influence in North America
- Upholding the nation's sovereignty

What was impressment?

Battle of Lake Erie

WAR AT SEA

Americans were proud of their victories over British warships on the high seas. But the greatest American naval victories of the war took place on the inland waters of Lake Erie and Lake Champlain. Oliver Hazard Perry's victory secured the Northwest, while that of Thomas Macdonough prevented a British occupation of upper New York.

BATTLE OF LAKE ERIE

Oliver Hazard Perry was given command of the naval force on Lake Erie in February 1813. Previous American defeats on land made control of the lake crucial for securing the Northwest Territory. On September 10, Perry unfurled his "Don't give up the ship" pendant on the *Lawrence* and led his ships into battle. After the British surrendered, Perry sent Major General William Henry Harrison the famous after-action report: "We have met the enemy and they are ours."

BATTLE OF NEW ORLEANS

In the last major battle of the war, Major General Andrew Jackson led a force made up of regular U.S. Army units, New Orleans militia, a contingent of former slaves, Choctaw Indians, Kentucky and Tennessee frontiersmen, and a colorful band of Jean Lafitte's pirates against British commander Edward Pakenham and his men. Jackson defeated the British in a lopsided victory.

A NATION EMERGES

For a small war that most people in Great Britain quickly forgot, the War of 1812 had great consequences for America. The defeat of the American Indians and the removal of the British and Spanish presence opened much of the continent for American settlement. It is impossible to imagine the same timeline of American growth, expansion, and national feeling if the United States had not gone to war, or if it had lost.

On August 24, 1814, British troops marched into Washington, D.C., and set the Capitol building and White House ablaze.

BATTLE ID

Battle of New Orleans

Battle of Lake Erie

Battle of New Orleans

STAR-SPANGLED BANNER

The original Star-Spangled Banner, the flag that inspired Francis Scott Key to write the song that would become our national anthem, is among the most treasured artifacts in American history.

MAKING THE FLAG

In the summer of 1813, Mary Pickersgill was contracted to sew two flags for Fort McHenry in Baltimore, Maryland: a large garrison flag (30 by 42 feet) and a smaller storm flag (17 by 25 feet). The larger of these flags became known as the "Star-Spangled Banner."

FLAG FACTS

- Made in Baltimore, Maryland, by flag-maker Mary Pickersgill
- Commissioned by George Armistead, commander of Ft. McHenry
- Original size: 30 ft. x 42 ft.
- Current size: 30 ft. x 34 ft.
- One of the flag's original 15 stars was cut out and given away in the 1800s
- Red "V" shape is an "A" sewn onto the flag by Louisa Armistead, widow of the commander of Ft. McHenry

How much was Pickersgill paid for the Star-Spangled Banner flag?

Mary Pickersgill

BOMBARDMENT OF FORT MCHENRY

On September 13, 1814, British forces began firing bombs and rockets on Fort McHenry in Baltimore Harbor. The bombardment continued for 25 hours. By the "dawn's early light" of September 14, 1814, Francis Scott Key, who was aboard a British ship several miles away, could just make out an American flag waving above Fort McHenry. British ships were withdrawing from Baltimore, and Key realized that the United States had survived the battle and stopped the enemy advance. Moved by the sight, he penned a poem that, when set to music, eventually became our national anthem.

FROM POEM TO ANTHEM

Inspired by the sight of the American flag flying over Fort McHenry, Key scribbled the opening lines for his poem on the back of a letter. The completed poem, first titled "The Defence of Fort McHenry," was printed with instructions that it be sung to the melody "Anacreon in Heaven." A music store subsequently published the words and music under the title "The Star-Spangled Banner." It became our official national anthem on March 3, 1931.

TRUE OR FALSE

T

F

EXPANSIONISM

During the 1800s, the United States expanded into western lands that had already been inhabited for centuries. As migrants came in search of wealth and better opportunities, they encountered and often clashed with Mexicans and Indians seeking to defend their homelands and traditional ways of life. Indians lost lands by treaties, wars, or failed agreements. The United States government pushed tribes in present-day Minnesota and South Dakota to the north and west. Surveyors mapped and divided the territory, turning it into saleable property. White settlers, encouraged by speculators, promotional broadsides, and government incentives, established settlements with hopes that land ownership would bring them prosperity.

MATCHING GAME

Touch a year on the left. Then touch the matching event on the right.

1829	Gold discovered in California
1838	Indian Removal Act passed
1830	Gold found in Georgia
1848	Trail of Tears begun

How many treaties were ratified between the United States and Native Nations?

Silver peace medal issued under President Thomas Jefferson and given to an Osage chieftain

EASTERN INDIAN WARS

Coveting what remained of the Indian lands in the Southeast and lower South, the United States forced tribes to cede their "rights of occupancy" and give up their ancestral homelands. After a series of bitterly fought wars, treaties and forced settlements divested Indians of millions of acres of land. Thousands of Cherokees, Chickasaws, Choctaws, Creeks, and Seminoles were forced to move west of the Mississippi.

In 1829, prospectors discovered gold in north Georgia on land that the Cherokee had long controlled. This newfound wealth was a major reason that whites demanded the eviction of the Cherokee.

Vignette on map of the State of Kentucky

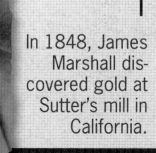

In 1848, James Marshall discovered gold at Sutter's mill in California.

TRAIL OF TEARS

In 1838, General Winfield Scott and U.S. Army troops began removing the remaining Cherokee in the South to present-day Oklahoma. Some Cherokee had gone west before the federal government began Indian removal, but most had remained. Men, women, and children were taken from their homes, herded into makeshift shelters, and forced to march or travel by boat over a thousand miles during a bitter winter. About 4,000 Cherokee died during the journey. Their forced removal, known ever since as the Trail of Tears, is among the most tragic episodes in American history. They were one of five major tribes forced to move west.

GOLD AT SUTTER'S MILL

The 1848 discovery of gold at Sutter's mill in California changed the wealth and reach of the nation. Farmers dropped their plows, sailors abandoned ship, and Chinese and others sailed across the oceans to seek their fortunes in mines and streams. These lands were often left devastated. Plentiful gold was minted into coins, made into jewelry, and financed the growth and statehood of California.

ESTABLISHING

In the 70 years following the American Revolutionary War, the United States expanded its borders to the Pacific Ocean and acquired more than two million square miles of contiguous territory through land purchases, treaties, and war.

President James K. Polk

POLK'S POLICY OF EXPANSION

President James K. Polk came into office in 1845 determined to acquire territory from Mexico. He believed that obtaining the sparsely populated Mexican land that stretched from Texas to California was critical to the future of the United States. The president hoped to purchase—not conquer—the land, but when Mexico rebuffed his advances, Polk ordered American troops under Zachary Taylor to march to the Rio Grande River, across land Mexico claimed. Violence erupted, and Congress declared war.

Map of the United States, 1839

BORDERS

Polk sent General Winfield Scott to capture Mexico City.

MEXICAN WAR

Texas's struggle for independence from Mexico and its annexation by the United States led to the Mexican War. From 1846 to 1848, the United States fought Mexico to acquire land stretching from Texas to the Pacific Ocean. President James K. Polk believed it was the nation's destiny to occupy these lands, and he planned an elaborate military campaign to seize them.

President Polk sent one army under Stephen Kearny to capture New Mexico and then march on to California. John D. Sloat assaulted California from the sea. Zachary Taylor attacked the main Mexican force from the north with a second army. All three U.S. attacks succeeded.

At the Battle of Cerro Gordo in 1847, General Winfield Scott demonstrated his effective leadership.

TRUE OR FALSE

T
F

Map of the United States and Mexico after the war

FRONTIER LIFE

The American West was dramatically reconstructed during the eight decades between the Mexican War and the passage of the Indian Citizenship Act in 1924. This period saw ever-increasing encounters between people of different cultural traditions and circumstances.

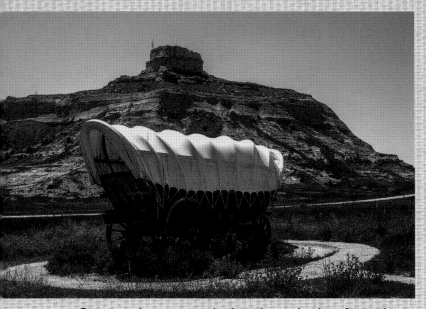

Covered wagons helped push the American frontier all the way to the Pacific Ocean.

LITTLE BIGHORN

At Little Bighorn (known to Indians as Greasy Grass), the U.S. Army suffered its greatest loss during the Western Indian Wars. On June 25, 1876, the army sent some 1,600 troops to trap a large group of roaming Lakota Indians and force them onto a reservation. Lieutenant Colonel George Custer, who led a body of 600 troops, thought he had enough men to defeat the Indians alone. The Indians greatly outnumbered Custer, and soundly defeated him and his five companies.

Battle of Little Bighorn (also known as Custer's Last Stand)

WHICH FRONTIER FIGURE?

Sharpshooter Annie Oakley was a major attraction in Buffalo Bill's Wild West show.

Brigham Young orchestrated the resettlement of the Mormon community to Utah.

Geronimo and his band of Chiricahua Apache fought government domination.

John Muir was one of the country's best conservationists, responsible for inspiring some of the country's earliest conservation legislation.

Sitting Bull gained a reputation as one of the most effective warriors during the three-decade-long military conflict between the Lakota and the U.S. Army.

George Custer was one of the most controversial military leaders in the West.

CIVIL WAR

Americans battled over preserving their Union and ending slavery.
Both sides envisioned easy victories after eleven Southern states seceded and war broke out in 1861. But the bitter, ruthless fight lasted four years.

THE ELECTION OF 1860

Republican Abraham Lincoln won the election of 1860 with less than 40 percent of the popular vote and without winning one Southern state. News of his victory prompted a secession movement across the South. By the time Lincoln took the oath of office, seven Southern states had formed the Confederate States of America. Four others soon joined.

The nation's bloodiest and most divisive war began at Fort Sumter in Charleston, South Carolina, on April 12, 1861.

BY THE NUMBERS

40

12,000

529,332

186,000

12,400

September 17, 1862, was the bloodiest single day of fighting in American history. Union casualties at Antietam were 12,400, including 2,100 killed; Confederate casualties were 10,320, including 1,550 killed.

Confederate General Robert E. Lee surrendered on April 9, 1865.

Confederate spy Rose O'Neal Greenhow with her daughter

ROLE OF WOMEN IN THE WAR EFFORT

Several thousand women worked as nurses in Union and Confederate military hospitals, caring for and comforting the wounded. Some women were commissioned, many volunteered; others were relatives of the wounded or members of private aid societies. Female spies for the Confederacy slipped in and out of Northern cities and Union strongholds, easily obtaining information on war plans. Vivandières—often the daughters or wives of officers—accompanied and provided support to many Union and Confederate regiments.

ROLE OF AFRICAN AMERICANS

At the outset of the war, the Union would not recruit African Americans, although escaped slaves, or contrabands, served in some units. But as the war progressed and casualties mounted, so did the need for more troops. In 1863, the Union began recruiting free blacks. By the end of the war, more than 186,000 African Americans joined the U.S. Armed Forces. Of these, an estimated 93,542 black soldiers were former slaves.

African American "contrabands" (escaped slaves) served the Union army.

LEGACY OF THE CIVIL WAR

President Lincoln was assassinated on April 14, 1865.

President Lincoln hoped that relations between the Union and the seceded states could be restored on the basis of reconciliation, not retribution. But Lincoln found himself at odds with Republicans in Congress. They wanted to punish the South for seceding and wanted Southern states to guarantee the freedom and rights of African Americans. Lincoln's assassination, and the ineffectual leadership of his successor, Andrew Johnson, enabled the Congress to control Reconstruction. They divided the South into military districts, withholding statehood from some former Confederate states until 1870.

WHICH AMENDMENT?

Thirteenth Amendment

Fourteenth Amendment

Fifteenth Amendment

African American men held elected office in every Southern state during Reconstruction.

EXPANSION OF RIGHTS

Among the most important legacies of the Civil War was the addition of three amendments to the U.S. Constitution, which ended slavery, guaranteed citizenship, and granted black men voting rights. The Thirteenth Amendment abolished slavery in 1865. The Fourteenth Amendment (1868) guaranteed African Americans citizenship rights and promised that the federal government would enforce "equal protection of the laws." The Fifteenth Amendment (1870) granted the right to vote to all male citizens, regardless of "race, color or previous condition of servitude." These amendments shifted responsibility for protecting rights to the federal government if states failed to do so. But racism delayed full implementation of the amendments and ultimately brought a new struggle for civil rights.

FREEDOMS DENIED

As soon as the war ended, many whites organized to oppose black freedom. Using terrorism and the courts, they forced African Americans away from voting booths and other public places. The rise of the Ku Klux Klan foreshadowed the difficulties that African Americans would face once the last federal forces withdrew from the South in 1877.

The Ku Klux Klan (KKK) was founded in Pulaski, Tennessee, to combat Reconstruction reforms and intimidate African Americans. They also intimidated the white population into non-interference.

SUFFRAGE FOR WOMEN

General Rosalie Jones (left) and Suffrage Pilgrims arriving in Washington, D.C., for National Woman Suffrage Parade

For more than a century, women in the United States struggled to obtain the right to vote. As they sought to claim their rights as citizens, they confronted prejudices against women's participation in political life. In 1920, the suffrage movement finally achieved victory with the ratification of the Nineteenth Amendment to the Constitution. Having won the vote, many women's rights activists continued to work toward a broader definition of social and political equality.

DECLARATION OF SENTIMENTS

Elizabeth Cady Stanton drafted the Declaration of Sentiments, a radical demand for equality that launched the first women's rights convention in Seneca Falls, New York. Modeled after the Declaration of Independence, Stanton's document proclaimed that "all men and women are created equal" and resolved that women would take action to claim the rights of citizenship denied to them by men. The Declaration of Sentiments was adopted officially at the Seneca Falls Convention in July 1848 and signed by 68 women and 32 men.

Suffragists Elizabeth Cady Stanton (seated) and Susan B. Anthony (standing)

Which state was the first to grant universal suffrage?

Suffragist Lucy Burns dropped leaflets over Seattle to advertise the upcoming National Woman's Party Convention in Chicago.

IMPRISONMENT

In the fight for suffrage, women were imprisoned for such "offenses" as holding open-air meetings and silently picketing the White House. While in prison, women were subjected to violence and intimidation, unsanitary living conditions, and were often placed in solitary confinement. When some of the suffragists instituted a hunger strike, they were painfully force-fed. Responding to increasing public pressure, the government eventually ordered that the suffrage prisoners be released from prison.

TRAVELING FOR SUFFRAGE

The path to equal suffrage would require multiple journeys and countless travelers from all across the country.

Suffragist Lucy Branham in Occoquan prison dress on the Prison Special Tour of 1919. The tour was possibly the most powerful use of travel to further the woman suffrage cause.

In 1917, militant suffragists staged a months-long vigil outside the White House.

SUFFRAGIST QUIZ

Rosalie Jones

Elizabeth Cady Stanton

Alice Paul

Betty Friedan

Mary Church Terrell

Judith Sargent Murray

INDUSTRIAL NATION

After the Civil War, the United States rapidly transformed into an industrial nation. Technological innovation, economic growth, development of large-scale agriculture, and the rapid expansion of big business characterized the era, as did social tensions brought about by immigration, financial turmoil, federal Indian policy, and increasing demands for workers' rights.

THE RISE OF BIG BUSINESS

The rise of big business created cutthroat competition for national markets. Faced with high fixed costs, businesses followed many strategies to prevent ruinous price battles. They created trusts and corporations. They merged with rival businesses and formed monopolies. They absorbed their suppliers or distributors. Kickbacks, bribery, price fixing, and secret deals were widespread. Americans debated the virtues and detriments of free enterprise.

DEBATING ENTERPRISE

Business and political leaders disagreed over the power of big business and whether it endangered the balance between private gain and common good.

Andrew Carnegie

"And while the law of competition may be sometimes hard for the individual, it is best for the race, because it ensures the survival of the fittest in every department."

Louis Brandeis

"We can either have democracy in this country or we can have great wealth concentrated in the hands of the few; but we can't have both."

Theodore Roosevelt

"The great corporations which we have grown to speak of rather loosely as trusts are the creatures of the State, and the State not only has the right to control them, but it is duty bound to control them wherever the need of such control is shown."

Early model of Singer sewing machine

THE SINGER STORY

Singer was one of the first big businesses. Although the sewing machine was a breakthrough technology, success took more. The company excelled at clever marketing. It opened factories and sales offices around the world. A vast new office workforce maintained control and profitability. By 1900, Singer was multinational. Singer Manufacturing pioneered many new business techniques. It instituted installment sales, sought to develop a home-user market, modernized manufacturing, and expanded into international sales.

LIGHTING A REVOLUTION

Many inventions in the late 1880s helped speed urban growth. One of the most dramatic improvements occurred in artificial lighting. Thomas Edison's development of an electric lamp that did not rely on open flames made lighting more practical and transformed city life. Edison's major contribution was understanding that the bulb was useless without an electrical infastructure upon which the bulb could work.

The introduction of the typewriter gave women the opportunity to enter the corporate workplace.

INVENTIVE AMERICANS

Touch a name on the left. Then touch the matching invention or innovation on the right.

Thomas Edison	Telegraph
Isaac Singer	Electric Lamp
Samuel F. B. Morse	Telephone
Alexander Graham Bell	Sewing Machine

Breaker boys, 1911

Haymarket Riot, 1886

Flint sit-down strike, 1936

LABOR MOVEMENT

As business got big, workers organized into unions to gain power and protect their interests. Unions negotiated the pace of work, the length of the workday, a less arbitrary hiring and firing system, safer workplaces, and a bigger share of profits. Unions benefitted from a growing working-class identity, but struggled with divisions based on skill, race, gender, and nationality.

Labor also confronted companies that used the courts, government, and violence to discourage workers from unionizing.

TRIANGLE SHIRTWAIST FIRE

On March 25, 1911, a fire broke out in the Triangle Shirtwaist Company factory in New York City's garment district. Locked doors and inadequate fire exits trapped workers inside, and the building's sole fire escape collapsed. Most of the

154 KILLED IN SKYSCRAPER FACTORY FIRE; SCORES BURN, OTHERS LEAP TO DEATH.

The World.

500 WORKERS, MOSTLY GIRLS, TRAPPED; BODIES OF DEAD HEAP THE STREETS; ONLY ONE FIRE ESCAPE FOR ALL.

mines, and mills. Employers liked to hire children because they could pay them low wages. Small fingers could reach into looms when fibers were stuck. Small bodies could squeeze into tight spaces in mines. Jobs were often dangerous, but many families needed the money desperately. The Fair Labor Standards Act finally set minimum age rules for child workers in 1938.

More children worked in the textile industry than in any other branch of manufacturing.

victims were female immigrants, some of which had only recently participated in an industry-wide strike to agitate for shorter hours and better conditions. The fire at the Triangle Shirtwaist Company factory became a national symbol of business neglect and abuse and galvanized the public resolve for workplace regulation.

CHILD LABOR

From America's earliest days, countless children contributed their work to building this country. In the 1800s, many American children worked in factories,

FAIR LABOR STANDARDS ACT

The Fair Labor Standards Act of 1938 established minimum wage, overtime pay, recordkeeping, and youth employment standards affecting employees in the private sector and in federal, state, and local governments.

DECLINE OF LABOR UNIONS

When organized labor reached the peak of its power in 1955, almost one-third of American workers were union members. Unionized workers enjoyed wages and benefits that gave them a greater stake in consumer society. Yet business interests and conservative legislators sought to dismantle unions through right-to-work legislation, erecting barriers to organizing workers and threatening collective bargaining.

LABOR MATCH-UP

Touch a year on the left. Then touch the matching event on the right.

1886	Fair Labor Standards Act passed
1911	AFL and CIO labor unions merged
1938	Haymarket Riot
1955	Triangle Shirtwaist Fire

COMING TO

Between 1880 and 1930, more than 27 million people made the journey to the United States from around the world. Immigrants came in waves, many to find work in the United States, and others to escape upheavals in their own countries. Ocean liners delivered immigrants across the Atlantic and Pacific to American shores.

Immigrants on an Atlantic liner

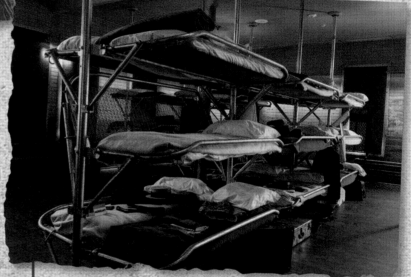

Angel Island Immigration Station

CHINESE EXCLUSION

The U.S. economy slowed in the 1870s, and competition for jobs increased. Chinese laborers faced growing prejudice and discrimination. In 1882, Congress passed an Exclusion Act, which barred Chinese laborers from entering the country and prohibited any Chinese person from becoming a citizen. Exclusion policies limited the numbers of Chinese voyaging to the United States from about 13,000 in 1880 to less than 2,000 a year in 1900. Those who still came had to prove they were not laborers. Of the Chinese people who came to the United States between 1850 and 1900, more than half returned to China.

ANGEL ISLAND

The Angel Island Immigration Station— known as the "Ellis Island of the West"— was the detention center for nearly half a million people who sailed through the Golden Gate to America. They came from China, Japan, India, Korea, the Philippines, Mexico, and Russia, among other countries. Like today, immigrants who sought

AMERICA

greater access to the United States wrangled with those who wanted more restrictions to keep them out.

IMMIGRANT LABOR

In the late 1800s and early 1900s, millions of immigrants came to the United States seeking greater freedom and economic opportunity. Most arrived with little money and took whatever jobs they could find. These massive waves of immigrants supplied much of the labor for the nation's industrial growth.

In many cities, recent immigrants converted small apartments into contract shops that doubled as living quarters.

TRUE OR FALSE   **T**
                      F

Ellis Island

AMERICAN RAILROADS

Dining car

Pullman porter making up an upper berth

LIVES ON THE RAILROAD

In the 1920s, railroads were a central part of American life. Railroad lines crisscrossed the country. They carried people, manufactured goods, food, the daily mail, and express packages. Railroads made long-distance travel possible, but the opportunities for travel were not equally shared. In the South, African Americans were segregated into "Jim Crow" cars.

PULLMAN PORTERS

In the 1920s, the Pullman Company was the largest single employer of African American men. From the 1870s through the 1960s, tens of thousands worked for Pullman as sleeping-car porters. The feeling of sleeping-car luxury came from the porter. He "made down" berths at night and "made up" the berths into seating in the morning, helped with luggage, shined passengers' shoes at night, and answered passengers' calls at any hour. Working 400 hours a month, porters earned better wages than most African Americans.

STREETCAR CITY

As electric streetcar (trolley) systems were built in the 1880s, 1890s, and early 1900s, American cities expanded. Many white city dwellers moved to new trolley suburbs; streetcars made it easy to travel greater distances to work, shop, and socialize in town. City streets and the patterns of people's daily lives changed. In Washington, D.C., streetcars turned outlying areas into new neighborhoods. Real estate developers often built streetcar lines to promote new suburban communities.

The broad streets in Washington, D.C., allowed the addition of electric streetcars more easily than did the narrower streets of many cities.

Streetcars connected Washingtonians to Center Market, the city's largest public market.

CENTER MARKET

Unemployed men outside a Chicago soup kitchen, 1931

GREAT DEPRESSION

In the Great Depression of the 1930s, Americans endured the greatest economic crisis in the nation's history. Like the American Revolution and the Civil War, the Great Depression was one of the defining experiences of the nation.

UNEMPLOYMENT

The depth and length of unemployment during the Great Depression was unique in American history. At its height in 1933, nearly 25 percent of the labor force was jobless. Unemployment stayed above 15 percent throughout the 1930s.

FINANCIAL CRISIS

In the late 1920s, banks ran amok—abandoning conservative standards to free up capital for risky investments. There were few government regulations to restrain them. By December 1930, banks were failing at an unprecedented rate. Citizens lost their savings; businesses lost the money they needed to operate.

The 1929 stock market crash triggered banking panics, as people rushed to withdraw their savings before they were lost. In March 1933, President Roosevelt ordered a four-day bank holiday to prevent further runs.

Drought and poor farming practices turned much of the high plains into a dust bowl.

DUST BOWL

In the 1930s, drought and intensive farming in the Great Plains brought about dust storms, crop failure, and human misery in one of the worst ecological disasters in America's history.

NEW DEAL

Franklin D. Roosevelt ran for president in 1932 on a promise to end the Great Depression and bring Americans a "New Deal." His "New Deal" programs to put Americans back to work began to reshape the public's attitudes toward government. It expanded the regulatory power of the federal government and the government's role in the economy.

During the Great Depression, government photographer Dorothea Lange took this picture at a migrant farmworkers' camp near Nipomo, California. "Migrant Mother" became a symbol for this period and had a dramatic effect on people.

NEW DEAL AGENCIES GAME

Works Progress Administration (WPA)

Social Security Administration (SSA)

Rural Electrification Administration (REA)

Federal Deposit Insurance Corporation (FDIC)

Securities and Exchange Commission (SEC)

WORLD WAR II

After the Japanese attack on Pearl Harbor in 1941, the United States joined the Allies in a global war that had been raging for nearly two years. By the end of World War II, more than 16 million American men and women had served, either as fighting forces or support troops.

AMERICAN-MADE WAR MATERIALS

Touch a number on the left, then touch the matching material on the right.

8,800	machine guns
2,600,000	trucks
324,000	warships
2,382,000	aircraft
20,800,000	helmets

We Can Do It!

As women were encouraged to take wartime jobs in defense industries, Rosie the Riveter became a celebrated symbol of female patriotism.

IMPERIAL JAPAN

After World War I, the U.S. emerged as the world's leading military power. But that didn't stop Japan. In an ominous prelude to World War II, Japanese forces swept into eastern China in 1937 and laid waste to Shanghai and Nanking. Japan's leaders proclaimed this the first step in creating a "new order" that would rid Asia and the Pacific of colonial influence.

NAZI GERMANY

Adolf Hitler and his Nazi Party swept to power in 1933. Immediately he began a vengeful and compulsive quest to remake Germany—and the world. He rebuilt Germany's war machine, mobilizing industry and expanding the military. As the Nazi *blitzkrieg*, or lightning war, raced across Europe, German forces committed unnumbered atrocities against the men, women, and children in their path. Most notoriously, the Germans undertook the systematic brutalization and mass murder of Jews, Gypsies, homosexuals, and others deemed "undesirable."

FASCIST ITALY

Benito Mussolini became prime minister of Italy in 1922 with dreams of restoring the glory days of the Roman Empire by conquering the Mediterranean. His military gains were limited to seizing easy targets: Ethiopia in 1936 and Albania in 1939. In 1940, as the German blitzkrieg spread across Europe, Mussolini allied himself with Hitler. He dispatched Italian forces to North Africa and Greece, hoping that an eventual German victory would enable Italy to claim these territories.

Adolf Hitler single-mindedly pursued his goals of military conquest and the elimination of Jews.

D-DAY

D-day was the launching date for Operation Overlord, the Allied invasion of Nazi-occupied Western Europe. In one of the most complex operations in military history, U.S., British, and Canadian forces landed simultaneously on five separate beachheads in Normandy, France, and stormed through intense German artillery fire to establish a foothold.

ON TOWARD BERLIN

In early spring of 1945, Allied infantry and armored divisions, in concert with a massive bombing campaign, pushed toward Berlin from both west and east. Millions of Allied troops advanced across Germany, breaking through German defenses. Along the way, they freed Allied prisoners of war. Allied forces also liberated concentration camps where Nazis had killed six million Jews and five million more "undesirables."

In the first week of May, following Adolf Hitler's suicide on April 30, the Nazi regime collapsed. Berlin fell to the Soviets, and Axis armies in Italy gave up. On May 7, 1945, Germany surrendered, and the war for Europe was over.

D-day invasion on June 6, 1944

U.S. infantrymen parading through Paris

JAPANESE

During World War II, almost 120,000 Japanese Americans, two-thirds of them American citizens, were forced out of their homes and into detention camps established by the U.S. government. Many would spend the remainder of the war living under armed guard, behind barbed wire.

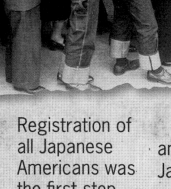

Attack on Pearl Harbor military base in Hawaii

BY THE NUMBERS

24

7

65

16

9066

10

Registration of all Japanese Americans was the first step toward forced removal.

EO 9066

Following the Japanese attack on Pearl Harbor on December 7, 1941, President Franklin Roosevelt signed Executive Order 9066, which resulted in the removal and imprisonment of Americans of Japanese ancestry.

REMOVAL

Temporary assembly centers were the first stop for most internees. Sixteen centers were established in California, Oregon, Washington State, and Arizona. Internees remained in these centers, under the control

INTERNMENT

of the Army's Wartime Civil Control Administration (WCCA), until the War Relocation Authority (WRA) camps were ready.

BEHIND BARBED WIRE

Japanese Americans were dispersed among ten WRA camps, located in seven states. The relocation centers resembled Army camps but were commonly below Army standards of living. Barbed wire fences, armed guards, and surveillance towers were common features in the camps.

MILITARY SERVICE

Some 25,000 Japanese Americans served in U.S. military units during World War II. The valor of these Americans, many of whom had family and friends living behind barbed wire, was extraordinary.

Their combat record aided the post-war acceptance of Japanese Americans in American society and helped many people to recognize the injustice of wartime internment.

Japanese American "evacuees" could take only those possessions they could carry.

AMERICANS AND AUTOMOBILES

With the introduction of the Model T in 1908 and the moving assembly line in 1913, the Ford Motor Company streamlined automobile production, transformed transportation, and kick-started American car culture. The assembly line meant that the company could produce more cars at less cost, making them more affordable. By the 1920s, the impact of the automobile affected everything from daily life to the economy to the environment. By 1930, 23 million cars were on the road, and more than half of American families owned a car.

4 CYL. MODEL T FORD, 1908
© the GROGAN PHOTO COMPANY Danville, Ill.

Model T

ROUTE 66

Route 66 was commissioned in 1926 and fully paved by the late 1930s. The highway linked the Midwest, Southwest, and southern California. Motorists and business owners adapted Route 66 for their needs and oriented their lives around it. Clusters of roadside buildings made Route 66 the "Main Street of America."

A slew of gas stations, tire shops, and garages sprang up to supply drivers' needs.

T
F
TRUE OR FALSE

Roadside attractions, hotels, gas stations, restaurants, and stores along Route 66 catered to tourists.

ON THE INTERSTATE

The Interstate Highway System, which began to take shape in the 1930s, was finally funded in 1956 with the Federal Aid Highway Act. The project called for over 41,000 miles of high-speed, limited access highways linking the nation's economic centers. The interstates changed commerce, travel, and where we live.

GAS CRISIS

To keep up with demand for gasoline, America began to import large amounts of foreign oil in the 1950s. In 1973, in response to American foreign policy in the Middle East, the Organization of Petroleum Exporting Countries (OPEC) placed an embargo on oil going to the United States. Almost overnight, gasoline supplies plummeted, and Americans learned first-hand the uncertainties and disruptions that could occur in a transportation system dependent on imported oil.

During the gas crisis in 1973, the government enforced rationing of gasoline. Depending on your license plate, even and odd numbers would alternate days at the pumps.

COLD WAR

After World War II ended, the United States and the Soviet Union began competing in a global struggle pitting democracy against communism. Tensions between the two led to such "cold" confrontations as the Berlin blockade, the downing of an American U-2 spy plane, and the Cuban Missile Crisis, while "hot" wars erupted in Korea and Vietnam.

REBUILDING EUROPE

In the struggle for control of post-World War II Europe, the United States used economic aid to support the democracies of Western Europe and stymie the territorial advances of the Soviet Union. Through the European Recovery Act of 1948, better known as the Marshall Plan, the U.S. poured more than $12 billion into Western Europe. Soviet leader Joseph Stalin criticized these plans, and the seeds of the Cold War were sown.

BERLIN AIRLIFT

The Berlin Airlift was one of the defining events of the Cold War. American and

Reconnaissance photos of Soviet missile sites in Cuba led to the Cuban Missile Crisis in October 1962.

TIMELINE

Touch a year, then touch the matching Cold War event.

1948	Berlin Wall opened
1949	Cuban Missile Crisis
1962	Soviet Union dissolved
1989	Berlin Airlift ended
1991	Marshall Plan signed

Fall of the Berlin Wall

British cargo planes delivered over 2.3 million tons of supplies to the citizens of Berlin during a Soviet blockade of the city from June 1948 to May 1949.

CUBAN MISSILE CRISIS

In October 1962, President John F. Kennedy learned that the Soviet Union was deploying nuclear missiles in Cuba. He demanded that the weapons be withdrawn and indicated his willingness to risk nuclear war if they were not. The crisis subsided only when the Soviets agreed to remove the missiles and the United States quietly removed similar missiles from Turkey.

FALL OF THE BERLIN WALL

During 1989 and 1990, the Berlin Wall came down, borders opened, and free elections ousted Communist regimes

President Truman pursued a policy of containment, bolstering any ally who stood in the way of Communist expansion.

everywhere in Eastern Europe. In late 1991, the Soviet Union itself dissolved into its component republics. With stunning speed, the Iron Curtain was lifted and the Cold War came to an end.

SEPARATE IS NOT EQUAL

In the mid-20th century, African Americans launched a renewed struggle to claim the civil rights that had long been denied to them. They moved to end racial segregation, calling on the nation to live up to its ideals of freedom, equality, and democracy.

SEPARATE BUT EQUAL

In 1896, the U.S. Supreme Court's decision in *Plessy v. Ferguson* ruled that racially separate facilities, if equal, did not violate the Constitution. Segregation, the Court said, was not discrimination. For the next half century, the doctrine of "separate but equal" was the law of the land.

WHAT YEAR?

FIGHTING UNEQUAL EDUCATION

Across the country, parents and community leaders fought against school segregation. In five different communities, African Americans from various walks of life bravely turned to the courts to demand better educational opportunities for their children. Case by case, their efforts began to undermine the legal principle of "separate but equal."

Alabama Governor George Wallace attempting to block integration at the University of Alabama

BROWN V. BOARD OF EDUCATION

In 1952, the Supreme Court decided to hear school desegregation cases from across the country. On May 17, 1954, the Court produced a unanimous decision to overturn *Plessy*. The Supreme Court's decision in *Brown v. Board of Education* stripped away constitutional sanctions for segregation by race, and made equal opportunity in education the law of the land.

1954   1896   1952   1957

MARCH ON

On August 28, 1963, work in the nation's capital came to a halt as thousands of demonstrators made their way to Washington. Around the world, millions watched on television as 250,000 people of different backgrounds came together to demand social justice and equality for all.

People arriving for March on Washington

PLANNING THE MARCH

On July 2, 1963, leaders representing six national civil rights organizations met at the Roosevelt Hotel in New York City to announce a march demanding jobs and freedom. In just eight weeks, they proposed to hold the largest demonstration in American history.

The concluding address was Martin Luther King Jr.'s "I have a dream" speech.

WASHINGTON

An estimated 250,000 people participated in the march.

President Lyndon Johnson signing the Voting Rights Act of 1965

MARCH LEADER ID

John R. Lewis

Roy Wilkins

A. Philip Randolph

James L. Farmer Jr.

Whitney Young

Martin Luther King Jr.

LATINO AMERICANS

Since the first Spanish explorers and settlers landed in the Americas, Hispanic people have shaped the history and culture of the United States and Latin America. Today, Hispanic and Latino Americans continue to demonstrate excellence in many areas including politics, public service, music, film, sports, business, science, and the military.

What is a *bracero*?

BRACERO PROGRAM

In 1942, facing labor shortages caused by World War II, the United States recruited Mexican men to work on U.S. farms and railroads in what became known as the Bracero Program. Between 1942 and 1964, an estimated two million Mexican men came to the United States on short-term labor contracts. A little-known chapter of American and Mexican history, the Bracero Program touched the lives of countless men, women, families, and communities. The bracero experience was one of exploitation but also of opportunity.

UNITED FARM WORKERS

In 1962, César Chávez held the first convention of the National Farm Workers Association, which later became the United Farm Workers (UFW). In 1968, amid growing talk

César Estrada Chávez, co-founder of the United Farm Workers of America, is one of the most recognized Latino civil rights leaders in the U.S.

TRUE OR FALSE

T

F

of violence among farm workers, Chávez fasted for 25 days to push for nonviolent actions. A keystone to the movement was a boycott of foods—especially grapes and lettuce—grown by companies with a record of poor rights for workers. These boycotts forced companies to expand farm workers' rights.

FLIGHT TO FREEDOM

The lure of economic opportunity and political freedom enticed many Caribbean people to attempt the risky journey to the United States aboard rafts and other flimsy vessels. Those arriving from Communist Cuba were generally given refugee status and allowed to stay, while most from Haiti and other impoverished areas were returned.

Art © 1973 Xavier Viramontes

VIETNAM

Americans fought a protracted and divisive war against Communist expansion in Southeast Asia. In 1956, President Dwight Eisenhower sent the first military advisors to bolster South Vietnam. By 1964, President Lyndon Johnson was deploying thousands of air and ground forces. Mounting casualties and an expanding draft fueled antiwar sentiment and deepened disagreements over the war's conduct and meaning.

Most Americans in Vietnam served as support troops and saw little combat, but "grunts"—the infantrymen on the ground—faced difficult conditions.

FIGHTING THE WAR

The war consumed Vietnam, a country not twice the size of Florida. North Vietnam was the target of repeated U.S. bombings, but South Vietnam was the setting for bombing, defoliation, and most of the fighting. The war also spilled over into Laos and Cambodia.

WAR

As casualties mounted and the draft expanded, antiwar sentiment and protests grew.

AMERICAN POWS

From 1961 to 1973, the North Vietnamese and Vietcong held hundreds of Americans captive in North Vietnam, and in Cambodia, China, Laos, and South Vietnam. Prisoners were often isolated, starved, beaten, tortured, and paraded in anti-American propaganda. While many more Americans were captured in previous wars, prisoners during the Vietnam War were a focus of public attention as never before. At the war's end, 661 of the 726 captured returned home.

BY THE NUMBERS

4,000

726

4

58,200

11,000

The Vietnam Veterans Memorial in Washington, D.C., was dedicated in 1982.

How many people with disabilities lived in institutions in the 1950s?

The Deaf and Dumb Asylum in Columbus, Ohio, which opened in 1829, was also a vocational training school.

DISABILITY IN AMERICA

People with disabilities and ideas related to disability are everywhere in American history. However, many stories and events related to people with disabilities never make it into the history books.

Wars create new generations of people with disabilities.

Woman operating a Braille machine

President George H. W. Bush signing the Americans with Disabilities Act

DISABILITY RIGHTS

The ongoing struggle by people with disabilities to gain full citizenship is an important part of our American heritage. The disability rights movement shares many similarities with other 20th-century civil rights struggles by those who have been denied equality, independence, autonomy, and full access to society.

POLIO

In the United States, polio was the most notorious disease of the 20th century until AIDS appeared. On April 12, 1955, it was announced that Jonas Salk, using March of Dimes donations from millions of people, had developed a vaccine to prevent polio. Today, polio vaccines have eliminated the paralyzing disease throughout most of the world.

TRUE OR FALSE

T

F

SEPTEMBER 11

On September 11, 2001, stunning attacks in the United States by al Qaeda, an international terrorist group, killed nearly 3,000 people and launched an American-led war on terrorism. The terrorists captured four American passenger airplanes, crashing two of the planes into the World Trade Center in New York and a third plane into the Pentagon. A fourth jet, bound for Washington, D.C., crashed in Pennsylvania, its hijackers thwarted by passengers.

Hijackers crashed an American Airlines Boeing 757 airliner into the Pentagon.

2001

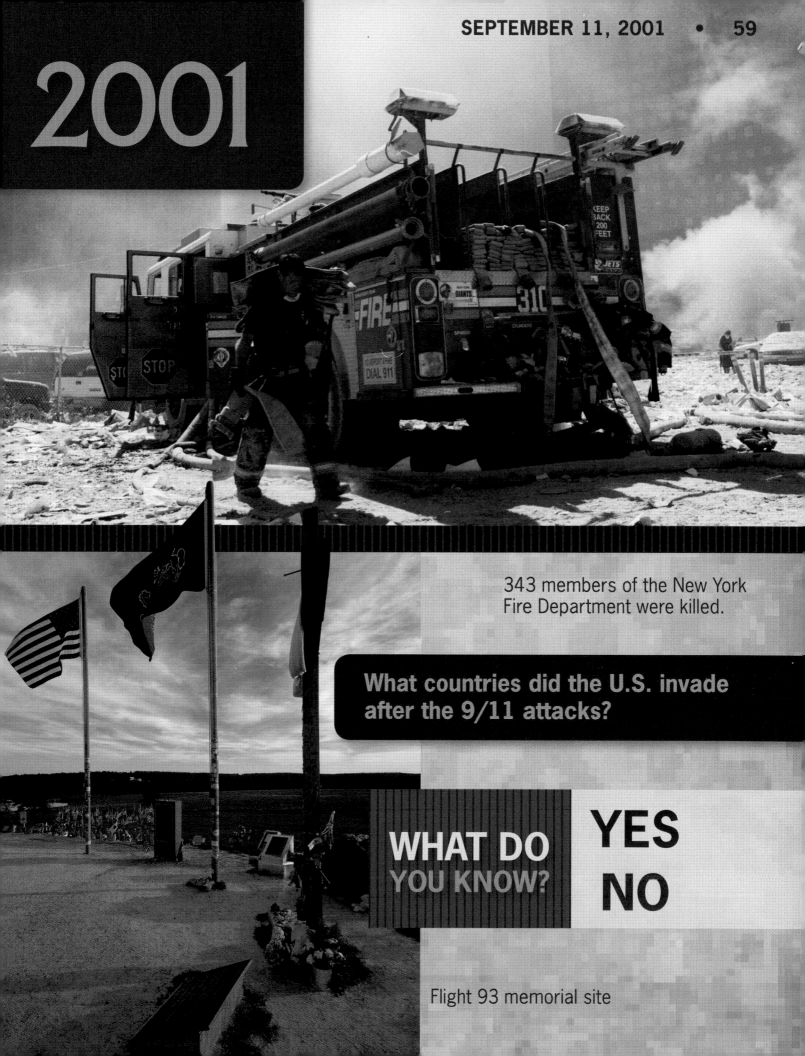

343 members of the New York Fire Department were killed.

What countries did the U.S. invade after the 9/11 attacks?

WHAT DO YOU KNOW?

YES

NO

Flight 93 memorial site

AMERICAN EXPERIENCE

Who assisted the Lewis and Clark expedition?

Sacagawea
Pocahontas

About how many Japanese Americans were interned during World War II?

120,000
16,000

What was the unemployment rate in 1933?

17%
25%

Who founded the United Farm Workers of America?

Roberto Clemente
César Chávez

When did women in the U.S. gain the right to vote?

1820
1920

When did the U.S. declare war on Germany and enter World War I?

1917
1927